The Make-Ahead Cookbook

2nd Edition

Over 50 Dinner Recipes You Can Make in Your Own Schedule (And Your Family Will Love)!

by Olivia Rogers

THE MENU AT HOME

Olivia Rogers
TheMenuAtHome.com

Table of Contents

Introduction

Many of us want to eat better but we just don't have the time or energy to cook after work. It's easy to give in to the temptation of delivery or unhealthy TV dinners after a long day at the office.

When you cook everything ahead of time and then just store it in the freezer, you can eat healthy, satisfying meals every day of the week.

Each of the 52 delicious recipes you'll find in this book are perfect for preparing ahead of time and freezing until you are ready to eat. For each recipe, you will notice that one step is written in italics. This means that if you are planning to freeze the meal for later, this is the step after which you'll store it in the freezer. If there are additional steps after, do those right before you plan to eat the meal.

1. Roasted Chicken with Honey Glazed Sweet Potatoes

The chicken and sweet potato provide a delicious combination of protein, fiber, and tons of essential vitamins.

Ingredients

- 4 whole Chicken Thighs

- 2 lbs. Sweet Potatoes (peeled, sliced)

- 1 Habanero Chili (minced)

- ½ cup Chopped Onion

- 4 cloves Garlic (chopped)

- 3 Tbsps. Apple Cider Vinegar

- 4 Tbsps. Honey

- 2 Tbsps. Olive Oil

- 1 Tbsp. Allspice Berries (ground)

- 1 Tbsp. Fresh Ginger (peeled, chopped)

- 1 ½ tsp Fresh Thyme (chopped)

- 1 tsp Salt

- 1 tsp Black Pepper

- 1 tsp Cinnamon

- ¼ tsp Nutmeg

- 2 Tbsps. Butter (melted)

- 1 Tbsp. Fresh Squeezed Lime Juice

- Mango Chutney

Method

1. In a processor, pulse together the apple cider vinegar, garlic, onion, allspice, thyme, ginger, chili, cinnamon, nutmeg, salt, and black pepper. Blend until pureed.

2. Place the chicken in a large zip lock bag. Add the marinade and seal. Turn and shake the bag gently to fully coat the chicken. Refrigerate overnight.

3. Preheat oven to 400° F. Place the chicken on a baking dish. Drizzle the marinade over it. Brush with olive oil. Bake for 45 minutes or until cooked through.

4. For the sweet potatoes: whisk together honey, butter, lime juice, and cinnamon in a large bowl. Add slices of potato. Toss until coated.

5. Arrange the slices on a greased baking sheet in a single layer. Bake them with the chicken until tender (about 25 minutes). Serve with mango chutney on the side.

Fun Facts

Here are 3 reasons you should be eating more sweet potatoes: They have a richer flavor but nearly half the carbs of regular potatoes. They are high in fiber and Vitamin A. Sweet potatoes are great for your skin, adding a youthful glow.

2. Mushroom Potato Gratin

A hearty serving of mushroom and potato provides you with a good helping of key essential nutrients.

Ingredients

- 2 ½ lbs. Potatoes (peeled, thinly sliced)

- 12 oz. Crimini Mushrooms (sliced)

- 6 cloves Garlic (thinly sliced)

- 1 cup grated Parmesan Cheese

- 1 ¼ cup Heavy Whipping Cream

- 5 Tbsp. Olive Oil

- 2 Tbsp. Fresh Thyme (chopped)

- 1 ½ tsp Salt

- ¾ tsp Black Pepper

Method

1. Preheat oven to 375° F (unless freezing). Grease a baking dish with 2 tablespoons olive oil. Add a layer of sliced potatoes and sprinkle with salt and pepper. Pour 1/3 cup cream over the potatoes.

2. Sprinkle with ¼ cup parmesan. Continue layering the ingredients in this way. Sprinkle thyme and garlic over the top. Bake for about 45 minutes or until potatoes are tender. Toss mushrooms in a bowl with oil, salt, and pepper.

3. Pour a ¼ cup cream and ¼ cup cheese over the top. Bake for another 20 minutes or until the edges start to turn gold and the mushrooms are tender. To reheat, cover in foil to prevent drying.

Tips

Use turnips in place of the potatoes if you are carb conscious. Add chicken or tuna for additional protein. Experiment with different sharp cheeses to land on your favorite flavor combination.

3. Meatball Mash

This takes the classic "meat and potatoes" to a delicious new level.

Ingredients

- 1 lbs. Ground Beef

- ½ cup Brown Rice

- 1 ½ cup Water

- 3-4 large Potatoes

- ½ cup Onion (chopped)

- 1 (15 oz.) can Tomato Sauce

- 2 ½ tsp Salt

- 1 clove Garlic (minced)

- 1 tsp Black Pepper

- 1 Egg

- ¼ cup Heavy Cream (or Buttermilk)

- 2-3 Tbsps. Butter

- 1 tsp Thyme

- 1 tsp Oregano

Method

1. Preheat oven to 350° F (unless freezing). Toss together ground beef, rice, onion, and ½ cup water in a large bowl. Add salt, pepper, garlic, and celery salt. Mix thoroughly. Form 1 to 2-inch balls with the meat.

2. In a large skillet, brown the meatballs and drain the fat. Combine tomato sauce and 1 cup water in a baking dish. Place the meatballs in the dish and roll to coat them in the tomato sauce. Cover and bake for about 45 minutes or until cooked through.

Tips

The rich flavor of this dish disguises the high nutrition value, making it the perfect dish for picky eaters. It's even better when served with a fresh salad on the side. Add 1 cup of rolled oats to the meat to add more fiber.

4. Smoked Turkey with Almond Mole

This dish is full of bold flavors that will make it hard to believe how amazingly nutritious it really is.

Ingredients

- 3 cups chopped Turkey Breast (cooked)

- ½ cup Roasted Almonds

- 1 (14.5 oz.) can Vegetable Broth

- 2 small Corn Tortillas (torn into bite sized pieces)

- 1 ½ cups Tomatoes (preferably fire-roasted, crushed)

- 1 (7 oz.) can Chiles in adobo sauce

- 2 dried Chiles (hot)

- 1 cup Onion (chopped)

- 2-3 cloves Garlic (minced)

- ½ tsp Olive Oil

- 1 Tbsp. Sugar

- 1 Tbsp. White Wine Vinegar

- 1/8 tsp Cloves (ground)

- ½ tsp Cumin

- ¼ tsp Salt

Method

1. Pulse almonds in a food processor until smooth. Set aside. In a large skillet, heat oil. Add chilies and sauté for 1-2 minutes. Add garlic and onion. Sauté for about 4 minutes. Add 1 canned chili. Leave it whole.

2. Add the tomatoes, broth, sugar, cloves, cumin, and salt. Bring to a boil. Reduce heat and simmer for 15 minutes.

3. Remove from heat and use a stick blender to blend until smooth (or spoon into the food processor). Return to heat. Add ground almonds and vinegar. Cook for 1-2 minutes. Stir in cooked turkey.

Tips

Use chicken or other poultry instead of turkey if not available. Add more or fewer chilies to taste. Use almond meal instead of whole almonds to save yourself a step.

5. Stuffed Chicken Rolls

Melted cheese and crunchy bread crumbs create bold combinations of texture in this dish.

Ingredients

- 4 Chicken Breasts (skinless, boneless)

- 1 cup Bread Crumbs (seasoned)

- ½ cup Parmesan Cheese (grated)

- ¼ cup Butter (melted)

- 1 (8 oz.) package Cream Cheese

- 2-3 cloves Garlic (minced)

Method

1. Preheat oven to 350° F (unless freezing). Pound chicken until thinned. In a bowl, combine bread

crumbs and cheese. Dip one side of each breast into the melted butter. Immediately dip the same side into the bread crumb and cheese mixture.

2. On the clean side of the breast, place 1-2 dollops of cream cheese. Roll them so that the cream cheese is on the inside. Secure with a toothpick. Bake for 40 minutes or until cooked through.

Tips

The melted cheese and crunchy bread crumbs make this the perfect dish for disguising a serving of veggies. Add carrot, spinach, or asparagus to the filing. Replace half the butter with olive oil for a healthier fat. Serve on a bed of brown rice or quinoa for added fiber.

Read This FIRST - 100% FREE BONUS

FOR A LIMITED TIME ONLY – Get Olivia's best-selling book *"The #1 Cookbook: Over 170+ of the Most Popular Recipes Across 7 Different Cuisines!"* absolutely FREE!

Readers have absolutely loved this book because of the wide variety of recipes. It is highly recommended you check these recipes out and see what you can add to your home menu!

Once again, as a big thank-you for downloading this book, I'd like to offer it to you *100% FREE for a LIMITED TIME ONLY!*

Get your free copy at:

TheMenuAtHome.com/Bonus

6. Juicy Make Ahead Ribs

Prepare this simple yet irresistibly scrumptious sauce and leave your ribs to marinate overnight in the fridge. Drizzle the rest over some rice!

Ingredients

- 4 lbs. Pork Spareribs

- ½ cup Honey

- ¼ cup Soy Sauce

- ¼ cup White Vinegar

- 3 cloves Garlic (minced)

- 2 Tbsps. Sugar

- 1 Tbsps. Molasses

- 1 tsp Baking Soda

Method

1. Preheat oven to 375° F (unless freezing). Cut up the ribs into single pieces. In a separate bowl, combine soy sauce, vinegar, honey, sugar, molasses, and garlic. Blend thoroughly.

2. Add baking soda and stir until it begins to foam. Dip the ribs into the bowl and coat thoroughly (until dripping with sauce). Cover a baking sheet with foil and arrange the ribs in a single layer.

3. Pour the remaining sauce over the top of the ribs. Cover with another layer of foil and bake for 1 hour or until cooked through.

Tips

Serve with a fresh salad or a side of quinoa to add more nutrition value. Keep these ready-to-go ribs on hand for spontaneous barbecues or dinner parties. Use low sodium soy sauce to keep your salt intake down.

7. Stuffed Lasagna Rolls

These single serving style lasagna rolls are easy, versatile, and perfect to freeze for lunches and dinners throughout the week.

Ingredients

- 1 (16 oz.) package Lasagna Noodles

- 1 (10 oz.) package Spinach (frozen, chopped)

- 1 lbs. Mozzarella (shredded)

- 1 (15 oz.) package Ricotta

- 2 cups Parmesan (grated)

- 1 lbs. Tofu (firm)

- 1 (28 oz.) jar Pasta Sauce (your favorite kind)

Method

1. Bring a large pot of water to a boil. Add lasagna noodles and cook until slightly underdone (about 5-8 minutes). Drain and rinse. Mix together mozzarella, parmesan, ricotta, tofu, and spinach in a large mixing bowl.

2. Lay a noodle flat. Spread a layer of cheese mixture across it. Then spread a layer of sauce on top of that. Roll the noodle up and place it in a baking dish (with the seam side down). Repeat this for all lasagna noodles.

3. Drizzle extra sauce over the top and grate a little extra parmesan over as well. Bake for about 30 minutes at 350° F (until bubbling).

Tips

Replace the tofu with squash, turnip, or sweet potato for more flavor. Serve with a fresh salad or a side of quinoa. Pair with a glass of red wine to boost heart health.

8. Prosciutto Wrapped Chicken with Pesto Pasta

This delicious and healthy dish is sure to impress even the pickiest of eaters. It's the perfect dish to come home to after a long day of work.

Ingredients

- 4 Chicken Breasts (skinless, boneless)

- 4 slices Prosciutto (large, thin)

- ¾ cup Goat Cheese (soft)

- 2 Shallots (chopped)

- 2 cloves Garlic (minced)

- 3 Dates (chopped)

- 1 Tbsp. Basil

- 3 large handfuls Fresh Basil

- 1 handful Pine Nuts

- 1 handful Parmesan Cheese (grated)

- 1 tsp Thyme

- Salt

- ¼ tsp Black Pepper

- Fresh Lemon Juice

- 1 (16 oz.) package Whole Grain Linguine

Method

1. In a food processor, combine 1 clove garlic, pine nuts, fresh basil, and a pinch of salt. Pour mixture into a bowl. Add parmesan and a little olive oil. Add just enough oil to create a gooey consistency. Add a squeeze of lemon juice. Set aside.

2. Grease a baking sheet with olive oil (unless freezing). Set aside. Heat 1 tablespoon olive oil in a pan on medium heat. Add shallots. Cook for about 3 minutes. Add thyme, salt, pepper, and garlic. Cook for 2 minutes.

3. Pour this mixture into a bowl. Add goat cheese, basil, and dates. Mix well. Slice a 1" slit into the thick side

of each breast. Use your fingers to expand this into a deep pocket. Stuff each pocket with the cheese and shallot mixture (about ¼ cup per breast).

4. Wrap each breast in a slice of prosciutto. Place them on the baking sheet (seam side down). Bake for about 40 minutes at 350° F or until prosciutto is crispy and browned.

Fun Facts

Each ingredient in this recipe packs a nutritious punch. It's the ideal balance of protein, fiber, and unsaturated fats. Basil is a natural remedy for upset stomachs and bad breath. Goat cheese is one of the few animal products that contains vitamin C.

9. Make Ahead Pierogies

Pierogies are wonderfully simple and extremely versatile. Modify this recipe to your own tastes.

Ingredients

- 3 cups Whole Grain Flour

- 2 cups Mashed Potatoes (cold)

- 1 (16oz.) package Sour Cream

- ½ cup Butter

- 2 large Onions (chopped)

Method

1. In a large mixing bowl, add sour cream and flour. Blend until it forms a dough. Roll the dough out on a

floured surface until very thin. Cut out 3 ½" circles. Add about a teaspoon of mashed potato to the center of each dough circle.

2. Fold the circle in half and press the edges with a fork. Set aside under a towel. Bring a large pot of water to a boil. Add the pierogies to the water a few at a time. Let them boil for about 4 minutes. Remove gently.

3. Melt butter in a pan on medium low heat. Add onions and cook for about 4-5 minutes. Add pierogies and cook about 3 minutes (until browned on the bottom).

Tips

Don't be afraid to experiment. Try any filling you can think of from sweet to savory and everything in between. Serve these on a bed of fresh salad for added texture and fiber. Use mashed turnip instead of potato for a lower carb alternative.

10. Almond Crusted Chicken Casserole

This simple casserole dish is a complete meal on its own.

Ingredients

- 5 cups Chicken (diced, cooked)

- 1 ½ cups Quinoa

- 3 cups Water

- 1 ½ cups Almonds (sliced)

- 1 cup Celery (chopped)

- 3 cups Cornflakes

- ½ cup Mayonnaise

- ½ cup Greek Yogurt (plain)

- 1 (10 oz.) can Cream of Mushroom Soup (condensed)

- 2 cups Chicken Broth

- 2 Tbsps. Lemon Juice

- 3 Tbsps. Onion (chopped)

- 1 (8 oz.) can Water Chestnuts

- 1 cup Butter (melted)

- 2 tsp White Pepper

- 1 Tbsp. Salt

Method

1. In a pot, combine quinoa and water. Bring to a boil. Reduce heat to low, cover, and simmer until the water is completely absorbed and quinoa is fluffy. Grease a baking dish. Set aside.

2. In a large bowl, mix quinoa, chicken, yogurt, mayonnaise, cream of mushroom soup, and broth. Add lemon juice, water chestnuts, onion, and 1 cup sliced almonds. Season with salt and pepper to taste. Pour mixture into baking dish.

3. In another bowl, mix the rest of the almonds, cornflakes, and melted butter. Spread on top of the

casserole. Bake for 40 minutes at 350° F or until browned and crispy.

Fun Facts

The almonds are rich in vitamin E which is great for your skin and hair. Greek yogurt is full of probiotics which helps improve digestion. The high fiber content in this dish also helps digestion and detoxes your skin.

11. Make Ahead Quiche

Quiche makes a perfect breakfast, lunch, or dinner. You can easily modify it to your own tastes.

Ingredients

- 1 (9") raw Pie Crust

- 1 ½ cups Swiss Cheese (shredded)

- ½ cup Ham (diced, cooked)

- 1 cup Milk

- 3 Eggs

- 4 tsp Whole Grain Flour

- ¼ tsp Salt

- ¼ tsp Dry Mustard (ground)

Method

1. In a bowl, combine flour and cheese. Spread this mixture across the bottom of your pie crust. Sprinkle in the ham.

2. In another bowl, mix milk, cream, and eggs together. Add salt and mustard powder. Beat until thoroughly combined.

3. Pour into the pie crust. Cover the crust in foil to prevent burning. Bake for about 1 hour at 400° F or until the filling sets.

Fun Facts

Despite the bad reputation, eggs actually lower bad cholesterol. Eggs are a superfood with a full range of nutrients in one tiny shell. Steep the egg shells in water for a day before watering flowers to provide essential minerals and nutrients to plants.

12. Sausage Manicotti

This hearty dish is simple and quick. It pairs well with a fresh salad and a glass of red wine.

Ingredients

- 10 Manicotti Shells

- 1 lbs. Turkey Italian Sausage

- 1 cup Green Bell Pepper (chopped)

- 1 ½ cups Onion (chopped)

- 2 cups Milk

- 2 cups Tomato Sauce (with Basil)

- ¼ cup Parmesan Cheese (grated)

- 1 ½ cups Mozzarella (shredded)

- 1 tsp Black Pepper

- 2 Tbsps. Whole Grain Flour

- 2 Tbsps. Butter (plus more for greasing)

Method

1. Boil manicotti shells until just underdone. Heat oil in a pan over medium high heat. Remove sausage from casing and add to pan. Crumble the sausage and stir until browned (about 5 minutes). Add onion and bell pepper. Cook about 5 minutes.

2. In a pot, melt butter over medium heat. Add flour. Cook 2 minutes, whisking constantly. Remove from heat and add milk while stirring with a whisk. Return to heat and bring to a boil. Cook until thickened (About 6 minutes), whisking constantly. Remove from heat. Stir in black pepper.

3. Pour ½ cup of this mixture into the sausage mix. Stir well. Spoon 1/3 cup of this mixture into each manicotti shell. Place manicotti on a greased baking dish. Pour remaining milk mixture over the manicotti shells. Sprinkle the mozzarella over the surface. Spread a layer of tomato sauce. Sprinkle parmesan cheese. Bake for 35 minutes at 350° F (or until bubbly).

Tips

Use shredded chicken as a substitute for turkey sausage for a different texture. Try different veggie combinations to keep this dish fresh and new. Replace ½ cup mozzarella with ricotta for a lighter, fluffier filling.

13. Onion Pepper Sausage Calzone

This highly versatile and surprisingly nutritious recipe can also be used for pizzas.

Ingredients

- 2 ¼ cups Whole Grain Flour

- ½ package Active Dry Yeast (about 1 1/8 tsp)

- ½ cup Warm Water

- ¾ cup Cold Water

- 2 Tbsps. Olive Oil

- 1 tsp Sugar

- 1 tsp Salt

- 1 lbs. Turkey Italian Sausage

- 1 large Onion (sliced)

- 1 Red Bell Pepper (sliced)

- 1 Yellow Bell Pepper (sliced)

- 1 ¾ cups Pizza Sauce

- 1 1/3 cups Mozzarella (shredded)

Method

1. Dissolve the yeast in warm water for 5 minutes. In a separate bowl, whisk together sugar, salt, oil, and cold water. Add yeast mixture. Add flour 1 cup at a time. Mix thoroughly until it begins to form into a smooth ball. Turn dough onto floured surface and knead for 5 minutes (dough should be smooth but still slightly sticky).

2. Divide the dough into 4 equal pieces. Roll each piece out in a rectangle (approximately 9" x 5"). Spread a layer of sauce over each piece. Leave a ½" border on all sides. Arrange sausage, onion, and bell pepper evenly on all pieces.

3. Sprinkle cheese over the tops. Fold the dough over lengthwise. Press the edges down with a fork. Bake for about 15 minutes at 500° F or until golden brown.

Tips

Prepare and freeze the dough in large quantities for spontaneous pizza or calzone nights. Stuff lots of different veggies into your calzone to make sure you are getting all your veggies for the day.

14. Hearty Chicken & Noodle Soup

This rich soup is easy to prepare and soothes the soul.

Ingredients

- 1 lbs. Beans (canned, borlotti or pinto)

- 1 lbs. Chicken Breast (cubed)

- 7 cups Chicken Broth

- 2 medium Onions (chopped)

- 2 medium Carrots (chopped)

- 2 stalks Celery (chopped)

- 5 cloves Garlic (minced)

- ¾ lbs. Pasta (preferably macaroni, penne, or other tube-shaped pasta)

- 1 tsp Black Pepper

- 1 tsp Rosemary

- 1 tsp Thyme

Method

1. In a large pot, combine chicken and broth. Bring to a boil. Reduce heat to medium, add carrots, onion, and celery. Let simmer for 15 minutes.

2. Add pepper, rosemary, thyme, garlic, and pasta. Let simmer another 10 minutes or until pasta is cooked.

Fun Facts

Beans are an amazing source of protein, fiber, and minerals. It should be a staple of any healthy diet. Garlic is a natural remedy for the common cold, flu, and other viral or bacterial infections. The beta carotene found in carrots helps protect your skin from sun damage and improves eye health.

15. Beef & Barley Soup

This rich and flavorful soup is perfect for fall or winter.

Ingredients

- 1.5 oz. Mushrooms (dried, chopped)

- 1 lbs. Beef (cross cut)

- 8 cups Water

- 1 large Onion (chopped)

- 2 large Carrots (quartered)

- 2 stalks Celery (cut into 1" slices)

- ½ cup Pearl Barley

- 2 ½ tsp Salt

- ½ tsp Black Pepper

Method

1. In a large pot, combine beef and water. Bring to a boil. Reduce heat to a simmer and leave it for 1 hour or until the meat is tender. Discard bones, fat, and gristle. Cut meat into bite-size pieces.

2. Return meet to water. Add mushrooms, onions, carrots, celery, barley, salt and pepper. Let simmer for about 40 minutes or until barley is tender.

Fun Facts

Barley is a great source of most vitamins and minerals. This soup is a perfect way to eat healthy on a budget. Carrots are actually more nutritious when cooked because your body can digest the vitamins more easily.

16. Mushroom Soup with Herbed Cream

This exquisite soup tastes like a 5-star restaurant recipe but is surprisingly simple to make.

Ingredients

- 2 lbs. Mushrooms (quartered)

- 3 large Leeks (diced)

- 6 cups Chicken Stock

- 6 Tbsps. Butter

- ½ cup Heavy Cream

- 6 Tbsps. Whole Grain Flour

- 3 tsp Thyme

- 1 ½ tsp Salt

- ¾ tsp Black Pepper

Method

1. Use an electric mixer to beat cream until it forms soft peaks. Add 2 teaspoons thyme and continue mixing. Cover and set in the fridge (between 2 to 24 hours).

2. In a large pot, heat 2 tablespoons butter. Add 1 lbs. mushrooms. Cook until lightly browned. Transfer to a large bowl. Repeat this process for the remaining mushrooms. Heat 2 tablespoons butter in the same pot. Add leeks.

3. Cover and cook until soft (about 5 minutes). Stir often. Add mushrooms. Sprinkle in flour. Stir until well mixed.

4. Add chicken stock, salt, pepper, and 1 teaspoon thyme. Bring to a boil. Reduce to heat to low and let simmer 20 minutes with lid halfway on. When serving, add a dollop of herbed cream to each bowl.

Fun Facts

Mushrooms are the only natural source of vitamin D aside from the sun (everything else is fortified). Multiple studies have found that mushrooms boost your immune system. Mushrooms are a great source of antioxidants.

17. Cozy Butternut Squash Soup

The full-bodied flavor of butternut squash is celebrated in this dish.

Ingredients

- 4 cups Butternut Squash (cubed)

- 1 cup Chicken Broth

- 1 (14 oz.) can Coconut Milk

- ½ cup Roasted Peanuts (unsalted)

- 1 cup Onion (chopped)

- 2 ½ tsp Red Curry Paste

- 1 clove Garlic (minced)

- 1 tsp Fresh Ginger (minced)

- 2 tsp Brown Sugar

- 1 ½ tsp Fish Sauce

- ¼ tsp Salt

Method

1. In a large pot, bring broth and squash to a boil. Reduce heat to medium and let simmer for 20 minutes (or until squash is tender). Add coconut milk, brown sugar, fish sauce, and salt. Let simmer another 10 minutes.

2. Heat oil in a pan on medium-high heat. Add onion. Cook 3 minutes. Add curry paste, ginger, and garlic. Cook 1 minute, stirring constantly.

3. Add curry paste mixture to the pot. Let simmer 10 minutes. Remove from heat. Use a stick blender (or food processor) to blend the soup until smooth. Spoon into serving bowls. Top with peanuts.

Tips

If you want to save time on this recipe, buy frozen pureed butternut squash. You'll need 2 12oz. packages. Roast the seeds in honey and salt for a scrumptious snack. Serve this dish with brown rice or quinoa for added fiber.

18. Herbed Pork & Beans

This variation on a classic will spice up your weekly menu.

Ingredients

- 1 cup White Beans

- 1 lbs. Pork Roast (boneless, cubed)

- 2 cups Chicken Broth

- 6 cloves Garlic (chopped)

- 2 cups Onion (chopped)

- ½ cup Water

- ½ cup Carrot (chopped)

- 1 tsp Sage

- 2 tsp Thyme

- ½ tsp Black Pepper

- ½ tsp Salt

Method

1. Heat 1 tablespoon oil in a pan. Sprinkle salt and pepper over the pork. Add to pan. Cook 6 minutes (brown all sides).

2. Add beans, broth, sage, thyme, onion, carrot. Bring to a boil then reduce to medium low, cover, and let simmer 40 minutes. Add garlic. Let simmer another 20 minutes.

Tips

Enrich the flavor by doing the beans from scratch. Put 1 cup of dry beans in a crock pot with 6 cups water and let it cook at a low temperature while you're at work. Use chicken instead of pork for a lighter option. Soak up the broth with a slice of whole grain bread.

19. Green Chili

Add a little heat to your menu with this delicious chili.

Ingredients

- 1 lbs. Chicken Breasts (boneless, skinless, cubed)

- 1 ½ cups Onion (chopped)

- ¼ cup Sharp Cheddar (shredded)

- 1 (15 oz.) can Kidney Beans

- 1 (15 oz.) can Tomatoes

- 1 (4 oz.) can Diced Green Chilies

- 1 medium Green Onion (sliced)

- ½ cup Salsa Verde

- 1 (12 oz.) bottle Dark Beer

- 5 cloves Garlic (minced)

- 1 Tbsp. Olive Oil

- 1 Tbsp. Chili Powder

- 1 tsp Hot Paprika

Method

1. Heat oil in a pan over medium-high heat. Add chicken. Cook until no longer pink. Add onion, paprika, and chili powder. Cook 4 minutes. Add garlic. Cook 1 minute. Add beer. Bring to a boil. Cook until liquid is almost evaporated.

2. Add salsa, beans, tomatoes, chilies. Reduce heat. Let simmer 30 minutes. Stir occasionally. Ladle into bowls and top with cheese and green onion.

Fun Facts

Here's 3 reasons to embrace spicy foods: Capsaicin (the ingredient that gives chilies their heat) boosts your metabolism, helping you lose weight. Capsaicin may reduce your risk of heart attack and disease. Some studies show it may even help fight cancer!

20. Rich & Hearty Pork Stew

This stew will warm you up while providing multiple servings of almost every food group.

Ingredients

- 1 ½ lbs. Pork Tenderloin (trimmed, cubed)

- 1 (28 oz.) can Hominy

- 2 ½ cups Chicken Broth

- 1 (14.5 oz.) can Fire Roasted Tomatoes (diced)

- 1 ½ cups Green Bell Pepper (chopped)

- 2 cups Onion (chopped)

- 1-2 cloves Garlic (minced)

- 1 Tbsp. Olive Oil

- 2 Tbsp. Chili Powder

- 2 tsp Oregano

- 1 ½ tsp Smoked Paprika

- ½ tsp Salt

- 1 tsp Cumin

Method

1. In a large bowl, mix cumin, paprika, oregano, chili powder, and salt. Remove 1 ½ teaspoons of spice mixture. Set aside. Add pork to the bowl. Toss to coat. Heat oil in a large pot over medium-high heat. Add pork and spice mixture. Cook until browned. Remove pork. Set aside. Add a little more oil.

2. Add onion, bell pepper, and garlic. Cook 5 minutes. Return pork to the pot. Add the 1 ½ teaspoons of spice mixture. Add broth, hominy, and tomatoes. Bring to a boil. Reduce heat, cover halfway, and let simmer 25 minutes.

Tips

Use chicken instead of pork if you're trying to cut red meats. Keep this stew seasonal by changing out the veggies with whatever's in season.

21. Guinness Beef Stew

The addition of Guinness to this stew adds a whole new dimension of flavor that will keep you coming back for more.

Ingredients

- 2 lbs. Boneless Chuck Roast (cubed)

- 5 cups Onion (chopped)

- 4 cups Beef Broth

- 1 ¼ cup Whole Grain Flour

- 1 ½ cups Carrots (sliced)

- 1 ½ cup Parsnips (sliced)

- 1 cup Turnip (cubed)

- 1 (11.2 oz.) bottle Guinness Stout (or other stout beer)

- 3 Tbsps. Olive Oil

- 1 Tbsp. Tomato Paste

- 1 Tbsp. Raisins

- 2 Tbsps. Parsley

- 1 tsp Caraway Seeds

- 1 tsp Salt

- ½ tsp Black Pepper

Method

1. Heat oil in a large pan on medium-high heat. Add beef and cook until browned. Remove beef and set aside. Add onion. Cook 5 minutes. Stir in tomato paste. Cook 1 minute. Stir in beer and broth.

2. Add the beef back in. Add salt, raisins, caraway seeds, and pepper. Bring to a boil. Reduce heat, cover and let simmer 1 hour. Stir occasionally.

3. Remove lid, bring to a boil. Cook 50 minutes, stirring occasionally. Add carrot, turnip, and parsnip. Reduce heat to low and simmer for 30 minutes or until vegetables are tender.

Fun Facts

Here's 3 reasons you want to add more dark beer to your diet: Flavonoids found in dark beer help break up blood clots. Dark beer is also packed with iron. A bottle of dark beer a day can reduce your risk of kidney stones by up to 40%.

22. Make Ahead Beef Rolls

These surprisingly healthy morsels will please the whole family.

Ingredients

- 6 cups Whole Grain Flour

- 3 tsp Active Dry Yeast

- 4 ½ Tbsp. Butter

- 4 ½ tsp Honey

- 2 tsp Salt

- 2 Tbsp. Milk

- 2 cups Warm Water

- 1 ½ lbs. Ground Beef

- 1 medium head Cabbage (shredded)

- 1 lbs. Mozzarella (shredded)

- 1-3 Chiles (hot, diced)

- 2 cloves Garlic (minced)

- 1 large Onion (chopped)

- Olive Oil

- Salt & Pepper to Taste

Method

1. In a bowl, combine warm water and yeast. Let sit 5 minutes. Add butter, honey, salt, and milk. Mix well. Stir in flour 1 cup at a time. Mix until a ball forms. Turn out onto floured surface. Knead until smooth (about 5 minutes). Cover with a damp cloth and set somewhere warm until it doubles in size.

2. Heat oil in a large pan on medium high heat. Add beef and cabbage. Cook until beef is browned. Add salt and pepper to taste. Divide dough into roll-sized pieces.

3. Flatten each roll and fill with a spoonful of beef mixture. Sprinkle cheese on top. Fold over and pinch the sides to seal. Brush the tops with oil. Bake for about 50 minutes at 350°F or until golden.

Tips

Try these alternatives to ground beef for an even healthier meal: Shredded chicken, Spinach and feta cheese, and Homemade tuna salad.

23. Black Bean & Sweet Potato Empanadas

The combination of black beans and sweet potatoes makes for an irresistible lunch or dinner.

Ingredients

- 2 cups Whole Grain Flour

- ¼ cup Cold Water

- 1 large Egg (beaten)

- ¾ tsp Salt

- 1/3 cup Olive Oil

- 1 Tbsp. Cider Vinegar

- 1 Tbsp. Cumin

- 1 cup Mashed Sweet Potatoes

- 1 cup Black Beans

- 1/3 cup Green Onions (chopped)

- 1 Egg White (beaten)

- 2 Tbsps. Cilantro

- 1 tsp Chili Powder

- ½ tsp Salt

Method

1. In a large bowl, combine flour and ¾ teaspoon salt. In another bowl, blend ¼ cup water, egg, oil, and vinegar. Gradually add water mixture to flour. Mix until it forms a ball. Wrap dough in plastic wrap and let sit in the fridge 1 hour. Toast cumin seeds in a pan over medium heat about 1 minute.

2. In a bowl, add cumin seeds, sweet potatoes, ½ teaspoon salt, black beans, green onions, cilantro, chili powder, and egg white. Mix well. Dive dough into 10 balls. Roll each ball out into a circle (about 5" wide).

3. Divide the filling evenly onto each dough circle. Fold over and press the edges down with a fork. Place them on a greased baking sheet. Cut 3 slits across the top. Bake for about 15 minutes at 400°F or until lightly browned.

Fun Facts

Black beans help speed up digestion which helps you lose weight. The high fiber content works to sweep out toxins from your system. Their high phytonutrient content helps lower cholesterol.

24. Make Ahead Samosas

Dip these rich and hearty samosas in sour cream, sweet & source sauce, or a fresh mint chutney for a simple yet wholesome lunch or dinner.

Ingredients

- 8 sheets frozen Phyllo Dough (thawed)

- 1 cup Mashed Potatoes

- 2/3 cup Frozen Peas (thawed)

- 2/3 cup Carrot (shredded)

- ¼ cup Onion (chopped)

- 2 Tbsps. Olive Oil

- 2 tsp Mustard Seeds

- 1 ½ tsp Garam Masala

- ½ tsp Salt

Method

1. Heat oil in a pan on medium heat. Add onion. Cook 2 minutes. Add carrots. Cook 2 minutes. Add peas, mustard seeds, salt, and garam masala. Cook 2 minutes. Mix in potatoes. Remove from heat.

2. Cut phyllo dough sheets into 3 strips (about 3"x14"). Spoon a portion of potato mixture onto the end of the strip. Fold that end over itself so that it forms a triangle shape at the tip.

3. Fold this triangle down. Continue to fold down until you reach the other end of the strip. Repeat for each samosa. Place samosas on a baking sheet. Brush with oil. Bake for about 20 minutes at 350° F or until lightly browned.

Tips

Make a large batch of phyllo dough from scratch to keep on hand for samosas and other yummy pastries. Use sweet potatoes, ginger, coconut milk, and cinnamon as filling for a sweet dessert. Get creative. You can stuff your samosa with just about anything.

25. Sweet Potato Burritos

These irresistible burritos are perfect for a quick lunch or dinner.

Ingredients

- 6 cups Kidney Beans

- 4 cups Mashed Sweet Potatoes

- 2 cups Whole Grain Flour

- 1 cup Warm Water

- 3 Tbsps. Butter (melted)

- 1 tsp Salt

- ½ cup Cheddar (shredded)

- 1 large onion (chopped)

- 4 cloves Garlic (minced)

- 2 cups Water

- 3 Tbsps. Chili Powder

- 1 Tbsp. Olive Oil

- 4 tsp Mustard

- 2 tsp Cumin

- 3 Tbsps. Soy Sauce

- Cayenne Pepper to Taste

Method

1. In a large bowl, combine flour, warm water, and melted butter. Mix until it forms into a ball. Divide into approximately 24 small balls. Roll out each ball into a flat circle (about ¼" thick). Cook each tortilla in a pan over medium-high heat until it bubbles up.

2. Heat oil in a pan on medium-high heat. Add onions and garlic. Cook 3 minutes. Mash in the beans. Gradually stir in water. Remove from heat.

3. Add soy sauce, cumin, mustard, chili powder, and cayenne pepper. Divide the mashed bean mixture and mashed sweet potatoes evenly among the tortillas.

Fold up the tortillas and place on a baking sheet. Bake for about 12 minutes at 350° F.

Fun Facts

Sweet potatoes are a fantastic source of most essential minerals. They help stabilize blood sugar levels which lowers the risk for diabetes and helps you lose weight. They also contain powerful cancer-fighting antioxidants.

26. Quick Wraps

These wraps are easy to make and extremely satisfying—perfect to take to work.

Ingredients

- 2 cups Whole Grain Flour

- 1 cup Warm Water

- 2 Tbsps. Butter (melted)

- 2 cups Brown Rice

- 4 cups Water

- 4 (15 oz.) cans Black Beans

- 2 (15 oz.) cans Pinto Beans

- 1 (10 oz.) can Whole Kernel Corn

- 1 (10 oz.) can Diced Tomatoes and Green Chilies

- 2 cups Cheddar (shredded)

Method

1. Follow the first 4 steps in the previous recipe to make tortillas with the flour, warm water, and melted butter.

2. Combine rice and water in a pot. Bring to a boil. Reduce to low heat, cover, and let simmer for about 20 minutes or until water is completely absorbed.

3. Transfer to a large bowl. Add beans, corn, tomatoes, chilies, and cheese. Mix well. Divide mixture evenly amongst the tortillas. Individually wrap each in plastic wrap. Heat in microwave for 2-3 minutes or until cooked through.

Tips

Try 2 or 3 different fillings to keep your lunches interesting. Swap corn for hominy to up the nutrition value. Swap quinoa for corn for even more whole grain benefits.

27. Cheesy Chive Loaf

This is the perfect bread to eat along with any of the soups in this book.

Ingredients

- 5 ¼ cup Whole Grain Flour

- 1 cup Warm Milk (about 100° to 110° F)

- 1 package Active Dry Yeast (about 2 ¼ tsp)

- 5 large Egg Yolks

- 4 large Eggs (whole, divided)

- ¾ cup Fontina Cheese (shredded)

- 1 tsp Sugar

- 3 Tbsps. Butter (melted, plus more for greasing)

- 1 ½ tsp Salt

- ½ cup Chives (chopped)

- 2 Tbsps. Water

- 2 Tbsps. Parmesan (grated)

Method

1. Combine yeast and warm milk in a large bowl. Let sit 5 minutes. Blend in butter, salt, and egg yolks. Stir in cheese and chives. Stir in flour 1 cup at a time until it forms into a ball. Turn dough out on a floured surface. Knead until smooth (but still slightly sticky).

2. Cover in a damp towel and let rise in a warm place until doubled in size. Beat 1 egg and 2 tablespoons water until foamy. Brush the top of the loaf with the mixture. Sprinkle with parmesan. Bake for 25 minutes at 375° F or until golden.

Fun Facts

Whole grains not only contain a high dosage of fiber but also a surprising amount of protein. Whole grains stabilize blood sugar levels protecting you from diabetes and other diet-related problems.

28. Buttermilk Whole Grain Pancakes

The whole grain provides fiber and flavor, making a hearty yet light and fluffy pancake.

Ingredients

- 1 ½ cups Whole Grain Flour

- 1 ½ cups Buttermilk

- 2 Tbsps. Butter (melted)

- 2 large Eggs

- 3 tsp Baking Powder

- 1 tsp Baking Soda

- 1 tsp Salt

- 1-3 Tbsps. Butter

Method

1. In a large bowl, combine flour, baking powder, baking soda, and salt. Add buttermilk, eggs, and melted butter. Mix until bubbly and free of clumps. Heat 1 tablespoon butter in a pan over medium-high heat. Ladle out pancake batter into pan.

2. Cook until the top begins to bubble then flip and cook the other side for 1-2 minutes or until cooked through. Repeat until the batter is gone. You may need to add another tablespoon of butter after every few pancakes.

Tips

Try adding any of the following ingredients right into the batter: 1 Banana (mashed, and an extra banana sliced for a topping), ½ cup Fresh Blueberries, and ½ cup Dark Chocolate (at least 70% cocoa, chopped).

29. Cherry Chocolate Cookies

Enjoy these scrumptious treats guilt-free because they are actually highly nutritious.

Ingredients

- 2/3 Cup Whole Grain Flour

- 1 ½ Cups Rolled Oats

- 1 tsp Baking Soda

- ½ tsp Salt

- 6 Tbsps. Butter (plus extra for greasing)

- ¾ Cup Brown Sugar

- 1 Cup Dried Cherries

- 1 large Egg (beaten)

- 3 oz. dark chocolate, coarsely chopped

Method

1. In a large bowl, combine flour, baking soda, salt, and oats. In a small pan, melt butter. Remove from heat, add sugar. Add butter mixture and egg to flour mixture. Mix thoroughly. Add cherries and dark chocolate. Mix well.

2. Divide dough into 2"-3" balls. Lightly grease a baking sheet with butter or olive oil. Press the balls onto baking sheet. Bake for 12 minutes at 350° F.

Fun Facts

The copper in cherries helps keep skin young and healthy. Cherries are high in vitamin C which helps your immune system. Studies have found that cherries help get rid of belly flab.

30. Supreme Lemon Pie

Makes 8 servings

Ingredients

- Nine-inch deep-dish pie pastry

For lemon filling:

- 6 tbsp. of corn starch

- 1 & 1/4 cups of divided sugar, granulated

- 1 & 1/4 cups of water

- 1/2 tsp of salt

- 2 tsp of lemon peel, grated

- 2 tbsp. of butter

- 1/2 cup of juice, lemon

For cream cheese filling:

- 3/4 cup of sugar, confectioner's

- 11 oz. of softened cream cheese

- 1 tbsp. of lemon juice

- 1 & 1/2 cups of thawed whipped topping

Method

1. Roll pie dough onto a lightly floured surface. Make a circle that is 1/8 inch thick. Transfer this to a nine-inch pie plate. Trim the pastry back and flute the edges. Refrigerate for a half hour.

2. Preheat your oven to 325F. Line the pastry with two layers of foil. Now fill the pastry with pie weights or dried beans. Bake on lower rack in oven for 20 – 30 minutes. Remove the weights and foal. Bake for 3-5 minutes more until the bottom has turned golden brown. Then use a wire rack to cool it.

3. For the lemon filling, you need to combine salt, 3/4 cup sugar and corn starch in a pan. Add water until the mixture is smooth. Bring the mixture to a boil on medium heat. Reduce the heat and then add the remaining sugar.

4. Stir and cook until the mixture is bubbly and thickened. Remove the mixture from heat and stir in

lemon peel and butter. Stir in the lemon juice gently. Cool until dish is at room temperature.

5. For the cream cheese filling, beat confectioner's sugar and cream cheese until they are smooth. Fold in the lemon juice and whipped topping. Spread filling over the pie shell and top with the lemon filling. Place in freezer-proof pan and freeze until needed.

31. Feta-Spinach Make-Ahead Feta Wraps

Serves 4

Ingredients

- 5 cups of baby green spinach

- 10 extra-large grade A eggs

- 1/2 pint of grape or cherry tomatoes, cut in half

- 4 whole-wheat, nine-inch tortillas

- Olive oil or butter

- 4 ounces of crumbled feta cheese

- Salt & pepper

Method

1. Whisk your eggs in a large sized bowl until yolks and whites are combined fully. Place a skillet on medium

heat and add sufficient olive oil or butter to coat the pan. When oil is hot or butter melted, pour in eggs and occasionally stir until the eggs have cooked completely.

2. Stir in a few pinches of pepper and a pinch or so of salt. Transfer eggs to a plate so they can cool.

3. Wipe down or rinse the skillet, put it back on medium heat and add more oil or butter. Add spinach and then stir often while cooking, until it wilts. Spread it on another plate and allow to cool.

4. Arrange the tortillas on your counter. Add about one-fourth of the eggs, tomatoes, feta and spinach in the middle of each tortilla and wrap tightly. Place them in a zipper-top gallon-sized bag until you're ready to eat them.

5. If you plan to freeze the wraps for longer than one week, wrap them in foil so they don't develop freezer burn. To heat, microwave at high level for about two minutes.

32. Oatmeal with Dried Cherries & Almonds

Makes 4-6 servings

Ingredients

- 3 & 1/2 cups of distilled or drinking water

- 2 cups of rolled oats, old-fashioned

- 1/8 of one teaspoon of salt

- 2 tbsp. of pumpkin seeds, shelled

- 1/3 cup of roughly chopped almonds

- 1/2 cup of cherries, dried

- Optional - sweetener, like agave, brown sugar or honey, to taste

Method

1. Grease a muffin pan and set it aside. Combine salt, oats and water in a saucepan. Bring it to a medium boil. Stir frequently as you cook, until the mixture is soft – about three to five minutes.

2. Mix in your choice of sweetener, if desired. Divide your oatmeal into muffin pan cups. Top with pumpkin seeds, cherries and almonds. Press lightly to push the toppings into the oatmeal.

3. Place muffin pan in your freezer until the oatmeal freezes completely. This will take three hours or more. Remove the pan and allow it to thaw a bit, until you can pop the oatmeal from the pan with a butter knife or spatula.

4. Wrap oatmeal pods in bags that are freezer-safe and replace in freezer. To serve, remove the number of pods you want and warm them in your microwave (in a bowl) for a minute or two.

33. Waffles & Cherry Sauce

Makes 6 servings

Ingredients

For Cherry Sauce:

- 10 ounces of frozen (not thawed) or fresh cherries, pitted

- 1 teaspoon of extract, vanilla

- 1 teaspoon of lemon juice

- 2 teaspoons of corn starch

- 1/4 cup of organic honey

- 1/4 cup of drinking water

For Waffles:

- 2 large Grade A eggs

- 1/4 tsp of salt

- 1/2 tsp of baking soda

- 1 & 1/2 tsp of baking powder

- 1/2 cup of meal, corn

- 2 cups of whole-wheat flour, white

- 2 tsp of vanilla extract

- 1 tbsp. of canola oil or olive oil

- 2 cups of non-fat or low-fat buttermilk

- 1/4 cup of brown sugar, light, packed

Method

1. For preparation of the cherry sauce: First, combine the cherries, vanilla extract, lemon juice, corn starch, honey and water in a saucepan. Bring this mixture to low boil over medium heat. Stir occasionally as you cook the mixture, until it has thickened. Set mixture aside.

2. For preparation of the waffles: Preheat the oven to 200F and place a baking sheet on center rack. Whisk baking soda, salt, baking powder, corn meal and flour in a bowl. Beat brown sugar and eggs lightly in a bowl. Add vanilla, buttermilk and oil and whisk until

they are blended well. Add wet ingredients to dry ones. Stir until they just become combined.

3. Preheat a waffle iron and coat lightly with a cooking spray. Add batter sufficient to cover 2/3 of waffle iron surface. Spread with spatula. Close the iron and cook the waffles for four or five minutes, until they are golden brown.

4. Transfer waffles to your baking sheet. This will allow them to remain warm. Make sure you don't stack the waffles. Repeat making waffles with batter. Add cooking spray when needed. Warm cherry sauce on medium heat until it is bubbly and hot.

5. To make ahead, prepare the cherry sauce, cover it and refrigerate it for no more than three days. Reheat to serve. Wrap waffles tightly. They can be frozen for no more than three months. Reheat in your toaster when you're ready to eat.

34. Cinnamon-Maple Applesauce

Makes 7 servings

Ingredients

- 2 sweet apples (like Golden Delicious) peeled and cut into one-inch pieces

- 6 tart apples (like McIntosh) also peeled, and cut into one-inch pieces

- 1/2 tsp of cinnamon, ground

- 2 tbsp. of maple syrup, organic

- 1/4 cup of drinking water

Method

1. Combine water and pieces of apple in a saucepan. Bring it to a medium boil, and then lower heat so the

apples simmer. Cover the pan and stir a few times while cooking, until apples become soft and fall apart. This usually takes about a half-hour.

2. Mash apples to your desired consistency and then stir in cinnamon and maple syrup. You can freeze this tasty treat for up to six months.

35. Mushroom, Asparagus and Potato Hash

Makes 4 servings

Ingredients

- 3 tbsp. of olive oil, extra-virgin

- 1 pound of baby or new potatoes, scrubbed

- 1 minced shallot

- 4 ounces of mushrooms

- 1 pound of asparagus, trimmed, cut into half-inch pieces

- 1/4 tsp of ground pepper, freshly ground

- 1/2 tsp of salt

- 1 tbsp. of sage, fresh, minced

- 1/2 cup of roasted, jarred red peppers, chopped

- 1 onion, small, chopped coarsely

- 1 minced garlic clove

Method

1. Place steamer basket inside a sauce pan. Add an inch of water – bring to medium boil. Lay potatoes in basket. Steam until just tender when pierced using a skewer. This takes between 12 and 15 minutes.

2. When the potatoes cool enough that you can handle them, chop them into pieces of about 1/2 inch each. Heat a tablespoon of olive oil in a skillet on medium heat. Then add garlic, shallot, mushrooms and asparagus.

3. Stir often as these ingredients cook, until they just start to brown. This takes about five minutes. Remove and plate. Add the rest of olive oil to your pan (about 2 tbsp.). Add potatoes and onion and stir while they cook. Scrape browned bits using a spatula until your potatoes brown, about five to eight minutes.

4. Return asparagus mixture to pan, with pepper, sage, red pepper and salt. Stir while cooking until they heat through. Place in freezer-safe bowl and freeze until needed. Reheat in the microwave.

36. Chicken & Veggie Fajitas

Makes 12 fajitas

Ingredients

- 2 pounds of skinless/boneless chicken breast, sliced

- One dozen flour tortillas

- 2 tbsp. of lime juice, fresh

- 1/2 cup of chicken broth, low-sodium

- 1 tsp of cumin, ground

- 2 tsp of chili powder

- 1 green bell pepper, sliced

- 1 red bell pepper, sliced

- 1 red onion, chopped

Method

1. Cook the skinless/boneless sliced chicken breasts in a skillet. Add 2 tbsp. of lime juice, 1/2 cup of broth, 1 tsp of ground cumin, 2 tsp of chili powder, the green bell and red bell pepper slices and the chopped onion.

2. Cook the mixture at medium heat until the vegetables become tender. Line up your 12 flour tortillas to prepare them for filling.

3. Spoon out 2 tbsp. of the chicken and veggie mix into the tortillas. Top with lettuce, guacamole, tomato, salsa, sour cream and shredded cheese. Wrap individually and place in freezer.

37. Chicken-Coconut Curry

Makes 3-5 servings

Ingredients

- 1 & 1/2 lbs. of chicken breast, sliced, lean

- 2 tbsp. of extra virgin olive oil

- 1 cup of chicken stock, low sodium

- 1 red pepper, chopped

- 1 onion, yellow, chopped

- 1/2 tbsp. of curry powder

- 1 tbsp. of sugar, brown

- 1/8 tsp of cayenne pepper

- 1 tbsp. of fish sauce

- 1 can of coconut milk, unsweetened

Method

1. Set a crock pot to medium. Add chicken breast, olive oil, onion, red pepper, chicken stock. Cook mixture until it is tender.

2. Add curry powder, brown sugar, cayenne pepper, fish sauce and coconut milk and combine ingredients. Allow to cook for four hours.

3. Remove crock from heat. Allow to cool. Add mixture to small containers (3-5) over rice. Place in freezer.

38. Creamy Chicken Soup

Makes 2-4 servings

Ingredients

- 1 lb. boneless, sliced, lean chicken

- 6 stalks of celery, chopped

- 2 carrots, medium, diced

- 1 onion, medium, diced

- 1 can of chicken broth, reduced sodium

- 2 cans of cream of chicken soup, reduced fat

- Egg noodles, couscous, rice or dried pasta

Method

1. Place chicken in a crock pot. Add chicken soup, chicken broth, onion, carrots and celery. Cook with setting on high for four hours.

2. During the last 30 minutes, add noodles, couscous, rice or pasta and cook until it is tender. Remove. Divide into containers and freeze.

39. Couscous Salad with Mustard Dill Dressing on Salmon

Serves 4

Ingredients

- 2 x 1/2-pound wild salmon filets

- Salt and pepper

- 1 thinly sliced shallot, medium

- 1/3 cup of olive oil, extra virgin

- Additional 2 tbsp. of olive oil, extra virgin

- 3 cups of vegetable broth, low-sodium

- 6 oz. of pearled couscous

- 2 tbsp. lemon juice from one lemon

- 2 tbsp. of Dijon mustard

- 1 & 1/2 cups of chopped spinach leaves

- 1/2 cup of roughly chopped dill

- 1/2 cup picked dill, roughly chopped, plus more for garnish

Method

1. Use salt & pepper to season the salmon. Heat 1/3 cup oil in a steel skillet on medium high until it simmers. Add the salmon with skin side facing down. Reduce heat to medium low.

2. Press down gently with spatula and cook salmon until skin is crisp and rendered. This should take 5-7 minutes. If the salmon skin shows any resistance when you try to lift it with a soft spatula, let it cook a bit longer until it will lift more easily.

3. Flip salmon over. Cook until thermometer in thickest portion reads 130F. Place salmon on a plate lined with paper towels and let it cool. Then flake it with your hands and discard the skin.

4. Wipe the skillet out. Add the 2 tbsp. of oil. Heat on medium high until it shimmers. Add shallot and one pinch of salt. Cook until the shallot has softened.

5. Add couscous. Stir while cooking, until it is fragrant and toasted lightly. Add the broth and stir to combine

the ingredients. Adjust heat as needed to maintain simmering. Cook until couscous becomes tender and most liquid is absorbed. Strain off excess liquid.

6. Mix lemon juice and mustard in a serving bowl. Stir in dill, spinach and couscous. Stir until spinach wilts and couscous becomes fluffy. Add in salmon flakes. Season using salt & pepper. Use dill to garnish. Place in freezer-safe container and freeze until needed.

40. Gruyère & Chicken Turnovers

Serves 4

Ingredients

- 1 & 1/2 cups of rotisserie chicken, shredded

- 1 & 1/2 cups of Gruyere, grated

- 2 thawed sheets of puff pastry, sold frozen

- 1 cup of peas, frozen

- 1/4 cup of Dijon mustard

- 1 beaten extra-large egg

Method

1. Preheat oven to 400 degrees F. Combine chicken, peas and Gruyere in a bowl. Cut puff pastry sheets in half, forming four rectangles. Place on baking sheet.

2. Top 1/2 of each single rectangle with chicken mixture, evenly. Fold the turnovers and seal them. Brush turnover tops with egg. Bake turnovers until they are golden brown. Allow to cool and wrap individually for freezing.

41. Braised Chicken Paprika

Serves 6

Ingredients

- 3 pounds of chicken pieces, bone-in (breasts, thighs and/or drumsticks) with skin removed

- 2 tbsp. of canola oil

- 1/2 tsp of pepper, ground

- 3/4 tsp of salt, coarse

- 1 pinch of granulated sugar

- 4 cups of onions, diced finely

- 1 tbsp. of salted butter

- 1/2 cup of sour cream, reduced fat

- 1 cup of chicken broth, reduced-sodium

- 1 tsp of marjoram, dried

- 1 tsp of red pepper, crushed

- 2 tbsp. of paprika, sweet

- 2 tbsp. tomato paste

- 1/2 cup of green bell pepper, diced

- 1 cup of red bell pepper, diced

- 2 tbsp. of fresh parsley, finely minced

- 1 tbsp. of flour, all-purpose

- Chives or dill

Method

1. Pat the pieces of chicken dry using paper towels. Season the chicken with 1/2 teaspoon of salt & pepper. Heat butter and oil in a Dutch oven or large casserole on medium heat. Add the onions and sprinkle the mixture with sugar.

2. Stir frequently while cooking until onions are light brown and very soft. Stir in the crushed red pepper, paprika, tomato paste and bell peppers.

3. Add in your chicken and stir it into mixture. Add the broth and sprinkle with marjoram. Cover pot with a lid that fits tightly. Simmer on medium low heat, just until the chicken is quite tender.

4. As chicken cooks, whisk the remaining salt and the flour and sour cream in a bowl until the mixture is smooth. After chicken is done, take it from pot and plate it. Stir sour cream and flour mixture into sauce. Allow to simmer and then cook. Stir until the sauce will coat your spoon.

5. Reduce to low heat. Put chicken back in sauce. Reheat the chicken and mixture for about one minute. After it cools, place in freezer-safe containers and place in freezer.

42. Black Bean & Sweet Potato Make-Ahead Chili

Serves 4

Ingredients

- 1 x 14 oz. can of tomatoes, diced

- 2 x 15 oz. cans of rinsed black beans

- 1/2 cup of fresh cilantro, chopped

- 4 tsp of lime juice

- 2 & 1/2 cups of water

- 1/2 tsp of chipotle chile, ground

- 4 tsp of cumin, ground

- 2 tbsp. of chili powder

- 4 cloves of minced garlic

- 1 onion, large, diced

- 1 medium peeled & diced sweet potato

- 2 tsp of olive oil & 1 tbsp. of olive oil

Method

1. Heat oil using Dutch oven on medium high heat. Add onion and sweet potato. Stir often as you cook this mixture, until the onion starts to soften, or about 3-5 minutes. Add salt, chipotle, cumin, chili powder and garlic. Stir constantly for 1/2 minute. Add in water and bring up to simmer.

2. Cover your pan and reduce heat, maintaining a gentle simmer. Cook until sweet potatoes are tender. Add lime juice, beans and tomatoes. Increase to high heat and then return to simmering, while stirring.

3. Reduce the heat. Simmer until mixture reduces slightly. Remove from the heat. Stir in the cilantro. Pour mixture into freezer-safe bowls and place in freezer until use.

43. Chick-pea Burgers with Tahini Sauce

Makes 4 servings

Ingredients

For chickpea burgers:

- 1 large egg

- 1 x 19 oz. can of rinsed chickpeas

- 2 tbsp. of flour, all-purpose

- 4 sliced and trimmed scallions

- 2 x 6 & 1/2 inch pitas, whole wheat, halved

- 2 tbsp. of olive oil, extra virgin

- 1/4 teaspoon of salt

- 1/2 tsp of cumin, ground

- 1 tbsp. of fresh oregano, chopped

For Tahini sauce:

- 1/4 tsp of salt

- 1/3 cup of flat-leaf parsley, chopped

- 1 tbsp. of lemon juice

- 2 tbsp. of tahini

- 1/2 cup of yogurt, plain, low-fat

Method

1. Place salt, cumin, oregano, flour, egg, scallions and chickpeas into your food processor. Pulse. Stop one or two times to scrape the sides down. Pulse again until the mixture is coarse but moist, and holds itself together when you press on it. Form the mixture into four patties.

2. Heat the oil in a non-stick, large-sized skillet on medium high. Add the patties. Cook until they are golden and starting to become crispy. Flip carefully. Cook until completely golden brown in color.

3. Combine the salt, parsley, lemon juice, tahini and yogurt in a bowl. Warm your pitas, if preferred. Divide patties among halves of pitas. Wrap and freeze until you want to enjoy them.

44. Sweet Potato Burritos

Makes 12 servings

Ingredients

- 8 oz. of cheddar cheese, shredded

- 12 x 10" tortillas, flour, pre-warmed

- 4 cups of sweet potatoes, cooked and mashed

- 3 tbsp. of soy sauce

- 1 pinch of cayenne pepper

- 2 tsp of cumin, ground

- 4 tsp of mustard, prepared

- 3 tbsp. of chili powder

- 2 cups of water

- 6 cups of kidney beans, canned, drained

- 4 cloves of garlic

- 1 chopped medium onion

- 1 tbsp. of vegetable oil

Method

1. Preheat your oven to 350F. Heat the oil in a skillet. Sauté garlic and onion until they are soft. Mash the beans into that mixture. Stir in water gradually and heat until mixture is warm. Remove mixture from heat. Stir in cayenne pepper, cumin, mustard, chili powder and soy sauce.

2. Divide the mashed sweet potatoes and bean mixture between your tortillas evenly. Then top them with cheddar cheese. Fold the tortillas like burritos around your filling. Place on a non-stick cooking sheet. Bake in oven until they are warm all the way through. Wrap burritos in foil and keep in freezer until you're ready to eat.

45. Cuban Vieja Tortillas

Serves 6

Ingredients

- 1 onion, sliced, small

- 1 x 8 oz. can of tomato sauce

- 1 cup of broth, beef

- 2 lbs. of steak, beef flank

- 1 tbsp. of vegetable oil

- 1 bell pepper, green, seeded, sliced

- 1 tbsp. of vinegar, white

- 1 tbsp. of olive oil

- 1 tsp of cilantro, fresh, chopped

- 1 tsp of cumin, ground

- 1 x 6 oz. can of tomato paste

- 2 cloves of chopped garlic

- Mashed potatoes with cream and butter

Method

1. Heat the vegetable oil over medium heat in a skillet. Brown your flank steak on both sides. It takes 3-5 minutes for each side.

2. Transfer steak to slow cooker. Pour in tomato sauce and beef broth. Add vinegar, olive oil, cilantro, cumin, tomato paste, garlic, bell pepper and onion.

3. Stir the mixture well until it is fully blended. Cover. Cook over high heat for four hours. Place in freezer-safe bowl(s) until needed. When you serve, shred the steak and serve with rice or tortillas.

46. Avocado Pork Tacos

Makes 6 servings

Ingredients

- 12 corn tortillas or taco shells

- 1 tbsp. of organic honey

- 2 tbsp. of lime juice, fresh

- 2 & 1/2 tbsp. of extra virgin olive oil

- 1 tbsp. of cilantro, chopped

- 2 cups of lettuce, iceberg, chopped

- Salt & pepper

- 3 radishes, small, sliced

- 1 tomato, large, diced

- 2 diced avocados

- 2 tbsp. of hot sauce

- 3 cups of pork, pulled

Method

1. Whisk olive oil, cilantro, honey, lime juice and one pinch of both salt & pepper in a bowl. Pour 1/2 of the dressing into another bowl. Add radishes and lettuce to one of the bowls and tomatoes and avocados to the other bowl.

2. Season the warm pork using hot sauce. Then divide the radishes and lettuce among the taco shells. Top them with tomato, pork and avocado. If freezing, keep mixture and meat separate from taco shells. Freeze mixture in a freezer-safe bowl.

47. Frittata with Lemon Chicken

Serves 6

Ingredients

- 2 tbsp. of lemon zest, grated

- 8 medium or large eggs

- 2 tbsp. of extra virgin olive oil

- Salt & pepper

- 1 & 1/2 cups of chicken, pulled

- 6 thinly sliced scallions

- 6 tbsp. of cheese, ricotta

- 3/4 cup of parmesan cheese, grated

- 2 cups of rice pilaf

Method

1. Preheat your boiler. Whisk 1/2 teaspoon of pepper and 1 teaspoon of salt with lemon zest and eggs in a bowl. Heat olive oil in non-stick skillet on medium high.

2. Add the scallions, then cool for two minutes. Add egg, pilaf and chicken. Scramble, folding the mixture over itself, until it is about 2/3 cooked.

3. Spread mixture evenly in your pan. Dollop ricotta cheese over it. Cook for one minute on low heat until the bottom layer sets. Transfer to your broiler and then cook for about three minutes, until mixture is golden. Sprinkle the top with the parmesan cheese. Cut mixture into wedges. Place wedges in freezer-proof bowl and keep in freezer until ready to serve.

48. Squash & Apple Rigatoni

Makes 6 servings

Ingredients

- 8 oz. of thinly sliced bacon

- 1 pound of rigatoni pasta

- 2 minced shallots

- 10 leaves of sage

- 3 cups of roasted, chopped squash

- 1/2 cup of Parmesan cheese, grated

- 1 sliced, tart apple (like a McIntosh)

- 1/4 cup of parsley, fresh, chopped

- Salt & pepper

Method

1. Cook the pasta until consistency is al dente. Then drain pasta, reserving one cup of the water it was cooked in. Using the same pot, cook the bacon just until it is crisp. Transfer bacon to some paper towels.

2. Add sage to the hot fat from the bacon and cook it until it is crisp. Transfer it to a plate. Add apple and shallots and cook together for five minutes.

3. Add parmesan, bacon, cooking water, squash and pasta and season with salt & pepper before tossing. Top with parsley and crumbled sage. Place in freezer-safe bowl until you're ready to eat.

49. Spanish Rice & Shrimp

Makes 6 servings

Ingredients

- 1/4 cup of olive oil, extra virgin

- 4 cups of rice pilaf

- 1 lb. of deveined, peeled shrimp

- 4 chopped garlic cloves

- 1 cup of tomato sauce

- 1 tsp of paprika, smoked

- 1/4 cup of black olives, chopped

- 1 cup of peppers, roasted & chopped

- 4 wedges of lemon

- 3 tbsp. of parsley, fresh, chopped

Method

1. Heat pilaf in two tablespoons of olive oil in a large skillet. Transfer the pilaf to a bowl.

2. In the same skillet, now cook paprika, garlic and shrimp in the other two tablespoons of olive oil. Add peppers and tomato sauce and cook until heated through.

3. Return the pilaf to your pan, add the olives and cook for one minute. Place in freezer-proof bowl(s) until you need them. Serve with lemon wedges and parsley.

50. Chicken Rice Mexican Soup

Makes 6 servings

Ingredients

- 3 cups rice pilaf

- 1 cup tomato salsa

- 2 tbsp. of cilantro, chopped

- 1 quart of chicken broth

- 1 & 1/2 cups of chicken, pulled

- 1/4 cup of lime juice, fresh

- 4 wedges of lime

- 1 medium avocado, sliced thinly

- 1/4 cup of sour cream

- 1/3 cup of Monterey Jack cheese, shredded

Method

1. Bring lime juice, broth and salsa to a boil in a medium sized pot. Divide the pilaf and chicken evenly into four freezer-safe bowls. Fill the bowls with broth, then top with cilantro, avocado, sour cream and cheese. Freeze until you're ready to eat. Top with lime wedges.

51. Baklava with Cashews

Makes 24 servings

Ingredients

- 1 & 1/2 cups of walnuts, chopped

- 1 & 1/2 cups of cashews, salted

- 1 tsp of cardamom, ground

- 1/2 cup of granulated sugar

- 1/4 tsp of allspice, ground

- ½ tsp of cinnamon, ground

- 16 sheets of phyllo dough

- 2/3 cup of melted butter

For syrup:

- 2/3 cup of water

- 1 & 1/3 cups of sugar, granulated

- 3 slices of fresh lemon

- 2/3 cup of organic honey

- 1/2 tsp of cinnamon, ground

- 2 cloves, whole

Method

1. To prepare the filling, combine allspice, cinnamon, cardamom, sugar, walnuts and cashews in your food processor. Cover. Pulse until the nuts have been chopped finely. Brush a large baking pan using some of your butter. Unroll the dough and trim it to fit inside the pan.

2. Layer four dough sheets in the prepared pan. Brush each one with butter. Keep the rest of your sheets of dough covered with a damp towel and plastic wrap so it won't dry out. Sprinkle with 1/3 of the nut mixture. Top with the rest of the dough, and brush each sheet using butter.

3. Cut the dough into 24 triangles with a sharp knife. Bake at 350F for 20 minutes or until the dough is golden brown. Combine syrup ingredients in a sauce

pan. Bring it to a full boil. Then reduce the heat, and simmer without a cover for about 10 minutes. Stir the mixture occasionally.

4. Discard cloves and lemon slices. Pour the mixture over pre-warmed baklava. Then cool on a wire rack until fully cooled. Cover and let it sit overnight. Place in freezer-safe container and store in freezer until you're ready to serve.

52. Crunchy Toffee Cheesecake

Makes 14 servings

Ingredients

- 2 tbsp. of sugar, brown

- 1 & 1/2 cups of graham crackers, crumbled

- 1/2 tsp of vanilla extract

- 1 cup of English toffee bits, milk chocolate flavored

- 1/3 cup of melted butter

For Filling:

- 1 cup of sugar, granulated

- 3 x 8-ounce packages of softened cream cheese

- 3 tsp of vanilla extract

- 8 ounces of sour cream

- 4 lightly beaten eggs

For Topping:

- 1/4 cup of sugar, granulated

- 1 & 1/2 cups of sour cream

- 1 tsp of vanilla extract

- 1/2 cup of English toffee bits, milk chocolate

- 1/4 cup of sugar, granulated

Method

1. Combine vanilla, butter, brown sugar and cracker crumbs in a bowl. Press this into the bottom and up the sides of a nine-inch greased pan. Set oven to 350F and bake for about 5-7 minutes, or until the mixture has set. Place on a wire rack to cool. Sprinkle with the toffee bits.

2. Beat sugar and cream cheese in a bowl. Beat in vanilla and sour cream. Add the eggs and beat on a low speed until they are barely combined. Pour this into the crust. Place your pan on the greased baking sheet.

3. Now bake at 350F for 45 minutes to an hour, until the center almost sets. Use a wire rack for cooling, for about 10 minutes. Run a knife carefully around the pan edges to loosen the baked mixture.

4. For the topping, combine vanilla, sour cream and sugar and spread this over the cheesecake. Bake for five more minutes. Set on wire rack to cool for an hour. Refrigerate for the night. Remove the sides of the pan. Place in freezer safe container and freeze until you're ready to eat.

Final Words

I would like to thank you for downloading my book and I hope I have been able to help you and educate you about something new.

If you have enjoyed this book and would like to share your positive thoughts, could you please take 30 seconds of your time to go back and give me a review on my Amazon book page!

I greatly appreciate seeing these reviews because it helps me share my hard work!

Again, thank you and I wish you all the best with your cooking journey!

Last Chance to Get YOUR Bonus!

FOR A LIMITED TIME ONLY – Get Olivia's best-selling book *"The #1 Cookbook: Over 170+ of the Most Popular Recipes Across 7 Different Cuisines!"* absolutely FREE!

Readers have absolutely loved this book because of the wide variety of recipes. It is highly recommended you check these recipes out and see what you can add to your home menu!

Once again, as a big thank-you for downloading this book, I'd like to offer it to you *100% FREE for a LIMITED TIME ONLY!*

Get your free copy at:

TheMenuAtHome.com/Bonus

Disclaimer

This book and related site provides recipe and food advice in an informative and educational manner only, with information that is general in nature and that is not specific to you, the reader. The contents of this book and related site are intended to assist you and other readers in your personal efforts. Consult your physician or nutritionist regarding the applicability of any information provided in our information to you.

Nothing in this book should be construed as personal advice or diagnosis, and must not be used in this manner. The information provided about conditions is general in nature. This information does not cover all possible uses, actions, precautions, side-effects, or interactions of medicines, or medical procedures. The information in this site should not be considered as complete and does not cover all diseases, ailments, physical conditions, or their treatment.

No Warranties: The authors and publishers don't guarantee or warrant the quality, accuracy, completeness, timeliness, appropriateness or suitability of the information in this book, or of any product or services referenced by this site.

The information in this site is provided on an "as is" basis and the authors and publishers make no representations or warranties of any kind with respect to this information. This site may contain inaccuracies, typographical errors, or other errors.

Liability Disclaimer: The publishers, authors, and other parties involved in the creation, production, provision of information, or delivery of this site specifically disclaim any responsibility, and shall not be held liable for any damages, claims, injuries, losses, liabilities, costs, or obligations including any direct, indirect, special, incidental, or consequences damages (collectively known as "Damages") whatsoever and howsoever caused, arising out of, or in connection with the use or misuse of the site and the information contained within it, whether such Damages arise in contract, tort, negligence, equity, statute law, or by way of other legal theory.

CPSIA information can be obtained
at www.ICGtesting.com
Printed in the USA
BVHW030254190819
556172BV00001BA/426/P